Bleeding Heart

Bleeding Heart

Poems by

Brandon McQuade

© 2021 Brandon McQuade. All rights reserved.
This material may not be reproduced in any form, published,
reprinted, recorded, performed, broadcast,
rewritten or redistributed without
the explicit permission of Brandon McQuade.
All such actions are strictly prohibited by law.

Cover design by Shay Culligan

ISBN: 978-1-954353-02-2

Kelsay Books
502 South 1040 East, A-119
American Fork, Utah, 84003

for Jacqlyn and Nolan

Acknowledgments

Grateful acknowledgments are due to the editors of the following publications where some of these poems, or versions of them, first appeared:

Elm + Ampersand: "Fledgling"

Vita Brevis: "Alzheimer's"

Rust + Moth: "Bleeding Heart"

College Green: "Sleeping Silence"

The Kindling Journal: "Nursing"

BlazeVOX: "Never Let Me Go"

Voices de la Luna: "The Sea Field"

*

I am forever grateful to my wife, Jacqlyn, for her support and motivation, and for being the first reader of all of these poems.

*

The phrase "precarious nest-cup" is from Michael Longley's poem "Swallows."

The title "The Sea Field" is Tom French's.

Contents

Electricity	11
Fledgling	12
Temporary Bedroom	13
Two Rooms	14
Alzheimer's	15
Bleeding Heart	16
Burial Site	18
Sleeping Silence	19
Nursing	20
Stillborn	21
Reflections	23
Winter in Wuhan	26
Never Let Me Go	28
The Sea Field	35
My Collared Shirts	38
Mango Seed	39

Electricity

We began like birds on power lines
in an age of innocence,
testing the electric charge
taking the path of least resistance.

She reached out her wing
to touch my own
or a neighbouring wire,
never fearing electrocution.

I slid like a worm along the line
never averting my attention
wary, all the while
of the current, consumption,
                                  or the fall.

Fledgling

I dream in the bed you were conceived
of the barn swallows outside our door
their precarious nest-cup hanging from the corner
a handful of mud and sticks in the beams.

Inside, eggs are hatching
the chicks are finding themselves
their eyes and legs coming down to earth
like the post-coital search for clothes and towel.

I realize, with my ear against her navel
listening to your mother like the mouth of a seashell
that the moment I cut the umbilical cord
my hands are forever responsible for your separation

your hand and mouth will reach for your mother's breast
as the fledgling foot escapes the nest.

Temporary Bedroom

Nolan McQuade, born January 6th 2020

We put together a temporary bedroom for you, inside our own,
your crib tucked neatly in the corner closest to your mother,
your playard doubling as a changing table and a wardrobe.
As your new voice calls for her in the night, seeking the comfort

of a quick cuddle or a long feed, I find it easy to almost forget
the nursery upstairs. You are growing so fast your clothes are kept
in three places: a bedroom for the present, another for the future
and a box in the garage for the past. I will always remember

your first days, when your head and neck needed me.
You bring us new life with every touch and giggle;
my son, you have shown us the meaning of unconditional
giving us everything, taking only what you need.

Two Rooms

Never will two rooms
be as full or as empty
as the waiting rooms
of palliative care and delivery.

A baby boy is born
his great-grandfather dead
a couple floors apart;
a family unsettled with the end
exonerated by the start.

Alzheimer's

i.m. Bernie McQuade

My grandfather stares at the flames in the propane fireplace
his palm wrapped loosely around a warm cup of coffee;
barefoot, he bares the soles of his feet
to the cold carpet, the colder floorboards underneath.

His eyes are deep blue, his hair a deeper gray
he stares at his reflection like the reflection of a ghost.
He remembers the farm, wheat fields and cold winters
forgets the names and faces of his children.

Bleeding Heart

The fog licks the surface
rolls in off the water
dense as dog breath
on a pane of glass

I watch the sun come up
the stars burn out
from this bed.
Like some old robot—

I am always plugged in—
nourishment and waste
plunged through IV and catheter—
every morning I read the newspaper

scan the obituaries
in search of my own name.
Every time I remember my wife
dying down the hall

I remember that I want to be dead.
My body haunts me
my bones creek and groan,
antediluvian.

My children come to visit
weeknights and weekends.
I used to tell time
by the sun on the crops,

the number of items left
on the hotel maintenance checklist.
These days I find myself
watching the clock

the skeletal arm and hand
ticking like a mechanical heart
the face a glass ribcage
like the ribcage of a dear

slowly bleeding
from a hook on the wall.

Burial Site

i.m. Yvonne McQuade

Rosary beads bind her wrists
like the purple veins bound
beneath her death-polished skin.

In a few days
her body will be laid to rest
in the everlasting shade
of her casket lid.

If I put one ear to the earth
the other to the sky
I can feel her soul lifted
her energy transmitted

in waves; soft whistles
through the weighted silence
of mud and stone.

Sleeping Silence

The foyer door of the
refurbished greenhouse
opens itself up like a seam
to plants, spiral staircases, trees

and the natural light
that shines between the beams
through the glass above,
down to the gleaming tiles.

The itch, scratch and ping
of the radiator within
Wintergarden Apartment
(number one-hundred & seventy-two)

like the faintest echo
of a distant car alarm,
the last gulp of *Guinness,*
a late-night sleeping-pill

or the soft scratches of eyelashes
against pillowcases—
these are the whispers
of waking-sleep.

Peaceful disturbances
of sleeping-silence
until the final sounds
are drowned in dreams.

Nursing

They have been following her ever since
she built a safety net under their nest
to catch the barn swallows falling.

Since the first signs and the positive test
her navel has grown firm, her breasts
sensitive and heavy. The barn swallows

keep busy, collecting mud and sticks
lined and hardened, like a palm print
on the tin roof of our patio light.

When she came home to find one
sprawled on her back, her premature wings
failing her, she placed her softly in her nest

while their mother looked away;
pretending not to know she can't neglect
nursing the children of her nest.

Stillborn

for Erin

This darkness that envelops me
has yet to show signs of light
but I'm still holding out hope
for someone to pull me out
by this cord—this slippery rope
that I hold now in my hand.

I know little of the outside world
because I have my own
here in this cozy little room
the warm, vacuum-sealed womb.
But you relay messages to me
telling tales of another home
in whispers and shivers from your bones.

Sometimes, while you soothe me to sleep
when everything is still, I can feel
the wet nose of a dog against your belly,
I kick and push to pet him through our skin
to feel his hair brush between my webbed fingers.

Sometimes, when you are sleep
and you think that I am fussing,
I am only trying to swim, kicking
to gain strength in preparation
for what will come on the other side,
beyond the narrowing walls of this room
in the world that I am almost ready for.

I will never experience the other world,
but I will rest forever in the red rivers of your body
and you'll be happy to know that I am grateful
knowing that a stillborn baby is born still
yet still born, loved, and never forgotten.

Reflections

I. Fledglings

Learning to fly is harder than it looks
for weeks now I have been finding fledglings
belly-up under the trees

their families mourning
from the branches above
swooping in anguish as people pass.

They grieve in singing voices
mothers and fathers in throat-swelling conversation
remembering their children

all the faller's fallen.

II. Waiting at the Locksmith

The water and the traffic pass along the Liffey
as I wait at the locksmith on the quays.
While I wait for a replacement
to the one I have lost, they build cylinders
and cut keys for doors still unmade.
The houses they will unlock are blueprints,
brick and foundation, their floorboards
still a concept. Further still, their doors—
a forest of trees: oak, pine, redwood, fir.

III. Winter

The soft snow faintly falling
is a sign of mourning
for all the dying and the dead
while my grandfather lays down to rest
lost in waking-sleep, in hospital bed.

IV. Fernhill Cemetery

i.m. Mya & Lexi McQuade

You are never afraid of darkness you never leave
is something I still dream
my stillborn sisters said to me

their bodies never knowing light
or anything of the deeper darkness outside;
every year my twin sisters hold hands

and walk the dewy grass of Fernhill Cemetery
to lay flowers on our sister's grave
on the morning of their birthday.

V. Burial Ground

i.m. Sonia Pye

Yesterday my grandmother was buried.
Five sons and five daughters in a circle around her;
as they lowered her body into the ground,
they remembered their mother and their father,

buried next to her. They gathered afterward,
their love burning in stories of varied length
like ten candles in my mother's backyard
while they slugged back drink after drink.

A widow of twenty years laid to rest
next to her husband at St. Augustine's
her burial ground reserved for two decades
like native land, a terminal for body and soul.

Winter in Wuhan

We met this pandemic in mid-November.
The beginning of the Chinese winter

in Wuhan. The sky was grey over the Yangtze
and the water was blue-grey.

Over the river, a cloud of evening bats
hangs in winged-silence

scouring the light above the lampposts
in pursuit of mosquitoes.

Far below, the lights of the Seafood Market
are switched off. Customers and proprietors turn in

like time-bombs, a swathe of targets
in the sightline and scope of the coronavirus.

The symptomatic cannot be treated and quarantined
before infecting friends and family

and those who show no signs, as of yet,
along with the asymptomatic

will carry on, their lives unchanged
booking flights and boarding planes

carrying sickness at a distance of six feet
from country to country.

The cruel irony of a disease fuelled and spread by the economy
in the Chinese pronunciation of bat or "fook"

being one and the same
as the pronunciation of prosperity.

Never Let Me Go

1

Hardened white film

mold

scale

at the bottom of the kettle

chips away

as the water boils
        like baked cheese on day-old dishes

2

Now and again

I want to collect these papers
       bundle these bridges I have built with words

rip

tear

shred them all
       and throw them all

out the car window

at near highway speed

3

Watch them float

ripple

in a swift current

tight pocket
       of rippling air;

in the brief moments
       before they madly flutter

aimlessly

toward the earth

I could almost change my mind…

reach out against
       the cold hard wind
              and pull them back

4

In the same moment
        that they're gone

(and I'm glad their gone
        I wanted them gone)

I will reach for them

I will stretch

reach

(even though I am glad they're gone—
        remember?
                It was me, myself, who wanted them gone)

reach out against
        the cold hard wind
                and pull them back

stretch

my arm against the angry wind

5

For these pages hold
      my friends and loved ones

letting me

go

as I let them

go

so I'll let them

go

if you'll let me

6

The black words
       are little black flies

on the white pages
       that grow white wings

they turn and look up at me

flapping
       madly

a great white heron

against the cold hard wind

7

It is the flies
        that open my eyes

finally

wake me

I am waken

to the pages shaking
        in my cold hard hand

and I reach out against
        the cold hard wind
                to pull them back

but they never left

no

they haven't

no

not yet

The Sea Field

I

The morning birds are telling us something
singing high over our neighbourly streets
drowning out the cicadas' painful screams.

They are singing for the unnamed, genderless dead,
the youthfulness taken on the brink of adulthood.

II

In the upstairs office where I write,
a painting hangs above the bookcase.
A framed Claude Monet we found at *Goodwill*—
Chemin dans les blés à Pourville.
It is yellow-gold and green-blue,
a path through a field of wheat
that leads to the cold blue sea.

Do you remember art?
Paintings, music, poetry?
What do the dead remember?
Your body will soon be washed clean,
your skin and veins cold and blue
as the sea in this painting.

III

We wash the dead one last time
then dress them in the finest suit and tie we can find,
or the finest blouse and pants. I have always wondered
why do the dead need clothes and footwear?
Especially those who are cremated.
We dress them up like they are going somewhere—
dead and on fire and underground—
we dress them up like they are attending their own funeral.
We cover the blemishes of death with make-up
to make them look presentable one last time,
for their loved ones to see them one last time.
We prepare them with love and care and due diligence
to meet, respectably, the faces they will meet in the afterlife.
But your loved ones do not get to see you die like this.
Only the doctors and the nurses and the mortician.
And your reflection in the bathroom mirror.
Your loved ones watch you die from a distance, behind a mask,
through hospital glass, a cold door or window.

IV

The birds fill our ears with songs of mourning.
The people of the neighbourhood mourn behind their masks
on the hot Texas summer morning of your death.

Birds have gathered on wires, rooftops and treetops
to sing down through branches and chimneys
with no regard for their own safety,
they do not practice social distancing.

But they sing for you, long and loud,
they sing joy and praise and love
and they welcome the cloud cover,
a cold shower in this drought
to wash and cool our warm bodies
like your body on its death bed,

the cool steel table where they make you look presentable,
the cold waters of the sea at the end of the wheat field.

My Collared Shirts

after Gerald Dawe's "The Good Suit"

My collared shirts hang behind the closet door
collecting dust and closet scent, waiting to be worn.

One is sweat-stained, another stained with spit-up;
one is faded, another worn thin in the collar,
but the red-checkered shirt is still in good shape.

When I put it on and button it up *(or is it down?)*
I disappear, the way my father used to disappear
after shaving his mustache, into another self.

When I button my shirt, part my hair to one side,
pull my glasses over my nose, and look into my eyes
I see my father in them, his father before him.

Mango Seed

Seated in his high chair like a king
my wife hands our son a mango seed.
He starts in on it, gnawing at the skin
with his six new razor-sharp teeth.

The skin of the mango never wears away,
not completely, no matter how hard he
tries. I remember my wife telling me
our energy must go somewhere when we die.

And then I think of the mango seed again,
how I have never believed in God,
or the soul, or the afterlife. But if there is one,
it must be like the skin of the mango seed
the last bit of energy clinging to our dead bodies.

About the Author

Brandon McQuade is a Canadian poet and a graduate of the University of New Brunswick and Trinity College, Dublin. McQuade is the poetry editor at *Montréal Writes*. He lives in Cheyenne, Wyoming with his wife, Jacqlyn and their son, Nolan. *Bleeding Heart* is his first collection.

www.ingramcontent.com/pod-product-compliance
Lightning Source LLC
Chambersburg PA
CBHW071642090426
42738CB00013B/3183